DAD JOKES

CHRISTMAS SPECIAL

101 of the best Christmas jokes ever!!

Illustrated by Ava Carlos

DAD JOKES
CHRISTMAS SPECIAL
101 of the best Christmas jokes ever!!

What do you call an obnoxious reindeer?

Rude-olph!

What happened to the man who stole an Advent Calendar?

He got 25 days!

Who delivers presents to baby sharks at Christmas?

Santa Jaws!

Where do Santa's reindeer stop for coffee?

Star-bucks!

How did Scrooge win the football game?

The ghost of Christmas passed!

What kind of motorbike does Santa ride?

A Holly Davidson!

What did Santa do when he went speed dating?

He pulled a cracker!

What did the snowflake say to the fallen leaf?

You're
so last
season!

What do you get if you cross Santa with a duck?

A Christmas Quacker!

What goes "Oh, Oh, Oh"?

Santa walking backwards!

How do Christmas angels greet

each other?

"Halo!"

Why does Santa have three

gardens?

So he can 'ho ho ho'!

What is the best Christmas present in the world?

A broken drum, you just can't beat it!

What do snowmen wear on their heads?

Ice caps!

What did Adam say the day before Christmas?

"It's Christmas, Eve!"

What do you get when you cross a snowman with a vampire?

Frostbite!

What did the stamp say to the Christmas card?

Stick with me and we'll go places!

Why did no one bid for Rudolph and Blitzen on eBay?

Because they were two deer!

Why don't you ever see Santa in hospital?

Because he has private elf care!

What do Santa's little helpers learn at school?

The elf-abet!

Why is it getting harder to buy Advent calendars?

Their days are numbered!

How did Mary and Joseph know Jesus' weight when he was born?

They had a weigh in a manger!

What do angry mice send to each other at Christmas?

Cross-mouse cards!

What's a dog's favourite carol?

Bark, the herald angels sing!

What does Santa do with out of shape elves?

Sends them to an elf Farm.

What do you call a bunch of chess players bragging about their games in a hotel lobby?

Chess nuts boasting in an open foyer!

What did the beaver say to the Christmas Tree?

Nice gnawing you!

Why did Santa's helper see the doctor?

Because he had a low "elf" esteem!

Who hides in the bakery at Christmas?

A mince spy!

How do snowmen get around

They ride an icicle!

What do snowmen have for breakfast?

Snowflakes!

What does Santa do when his elves misbehave?

He gives them the sack!

What did Santa say to the smoker?

Please don't smoke, it's bad for my elf!

What do you get if you eat
Christmas decorations?

Tinsilitis!

**What's green, covered in tinsel
and goes ribbet ribbet?**

A mistle-toad!

What carol is heard in the desert?

'O camel ye faithful!'

How many letters are in the Christmas alphabet?

Only 25, there's no L!

What do reindeer hang on their Christmas trees?

Horn-aments!

Why are Christmas trees so bad at sewing?

They always drop their needles!

How does Christmas Day end?

With the letter Y!

What happened to the turkey at Christmas?

It got gobbled!

Who's Rudolph's favourite pop star?

Beyon-sleigh!

When is a boat just like snow

When it's adrift!

Who delivers presents to cats?

Santa Paws!

Why did the turkey cross the road?

Because it was the chicken's day off!

What do you get if you cross Santa with a detective?

Santa Clues!

What goes Ho Ho Whoosh, Ho Ho Whoosh?

Santa going through a revolving door!

What is Santa's favourite place to deliver presents?

Idaho-ho-ho!

What do you call buying a piano for the holidays?

Christmas Chopin!

What's a child's favourite king at Christmas?

A stoc-king!

Who is Santa's favourite singer?

Elf-is Presley!

Why couldn't the skeleton go to the Christmas Party?

Because he had no body to go with!

How does Darth Vader enjoy his Christmas Turkey?

On the dark side!

What do snowmen eat for lunch?

Icebergers!

What is Santa's first language?

North Polish.

Why are Christmas trees so fond of the past?

Because the present's beneath them!

How do you lift a frozen car?

With a Jack Frost!

Who is a Christmas tree's favourite singer?

Spruce Springsteen!

What cars do elves drive?

Toyotas!

What do monkeys sing at Christmas?

Jungle bells!

What do reindeer say before they tell a joke?

This one will sleigh you!

Why did Scrooge keep a pet lamb?

Because it would say, "Baaaaahh humbug!"

Which holiday mascot has the least spare change?

St. Nickel-less!

What would you call an elf who just has won the lottery?

Welfy!

What is white and minty?

A polo bear!

What do the elves cook with in the kitchen?

Utinsels!

How did the bauble get addicted to Christmas?

He was hooked on trees his whole life!

What do you call a kid who doesn't believe in Santa?

A rebel without a Claus!

Why does Santa go down the chimney?

Because it soots him!

What does Santa suffer from if he gets stuck in a chimney?

Claus-trophobia!

Why did Santa get a parking ticket on Christmas Eve?

He left his sleigh in a snow parking zone!

What do you call Santa living at the South Pole?

A lost Claus!

What part of the body do you only see during Christmas?

Mistletoe!

What athlete is warmest in winter?

A long jumper!

What do you call a snowman with a six pack?

An abdominal snowman!

What do you call cutting down a Christmas tree?

Christmas chopping!

What do sheep say at Christmas?

A Merry Christmas to Ewe!

What did Mrs. Claus say to Santa Claus when she looked up in the sky?

Looks like rain, dear!

Which football team did the baby Jesus support?

Manger-ster United!

What do you get if you cross a Christmas tree with an apple?

A pine-apple!

Why is winter a snowman's favourite time of year?

Because they can camouflage!

What do vampires sing on New Year's Eve?

Auld Fang Syne!

Why is everyone so thirsty at the North Pole?

There's no well, no well!

What do you get if you cross a bell with a skunk?

Jingle Smells!

What do you get when you cross a deer with rain?

A reindeer!

What's worse than Rudolph with a runny nose?

Frosty the Snowman with a hot flush!

Knock, knock. Who's there? **Arthur.** Arthur who? **Arthur any mince pies left?**

What do they sing at a snowman's birthday party?

Freeze a jolly good fellow!

What's Santa Claus's favourite sport?

North Pole-vaulting!

What do you call Rudolph with lots of snow in his ears?

Anything you want, he can't hear you!

Why are horse-drawn carriages so unpopular?

Because horses are rubbish at drawing!

Why are turkeys always in rock bands?

Because they have drumsticks!

What does Miley Cyrus have at Christmas?

Twerky!

Where do Christmas plants go when they want to become movie stars?

Holly-wood!

What kind of Christmas music do elves like?

"Wrap" music!

What's Jack Frost's favourite part of the school day?

Snow and tell.

Why was the snowman rummaging in a bag of carrots?

He was picking his nose!

What's a mathematician's favourite Christmas snack?

A mince pi

What's red and white and falls down chimneys?

Santa Klutz!

What's the difference between Santa Claus and a knight?

One slays a dragon, the other drags a sleigh!

What happened when the snowgirl fell out with the snowboy?

She gave him the cold shoulder!

Hope you enjoyed this book..

If you did, please leave a 5 Star review on Amazon.

For every 5 Star review we get, we will donate a slice of the book's proceeds to charity this holiday season!